Thinking about the Seasons

Summer

Clare Collinson

W
FRANKLIN WATTS
NEW YORK • LONDON • SYDNEY

D0537952

700033747370

This edition 2013

Franklin Watts
338 Euston Road
London NW1 3BH

Franklin Watts Australia
Level 17/207 Kent Street
Sydney NSW 2000

ISBN: 978 1 4451 1965 6

Dewey classification number: 508.2

A CIP catalogue record for this book is available
from the British Library.

Planning and production by Discovery Books Limited
Managing editor: Laura Durman
Editor: Clare Collinson
Picture researcher: Rachel Tisdale
Designer: Ian Winton

Photographs: Chris Fairclough: p. 4, 9; Getty Images: title page (Kane Skennar), p. 8 (P. Broze & A. Chederros),
p. 10 (Ariel Skelley), p. 11 (Leon Giran-Max/Fine Art Photographic), p. 18 (Imagno), p. 20 (Michelle Quance), p. 22
(Larry Dale Gordon), p. 23 (Image Source), p. 24 (Flying Colours Ltd), p. 26 (Gregory Costanzo), p. 28 (Bigshots),
p. 29 (Brian Summers), p. 30 (English School); istockphoto.com: p. 5 (Tinas Bercic), p. 6 (Nathan Gleave), p. 7 (Chan
Pak Kei), p. 12 (Adam Tinney), p. 14 (Jello5700), p. 16 (Can Balcioglu), p. 17 (Ali-Lan Lee), p. 19 (Tony Svensson),
p. 21 (Joselito Briones), p. 25 (Chutima Chokkij), p. 31 (Josef Philipp); Shutterstock Images: p. 15 (Jean Frooms)

Cover photos: istockphoto.com: Jacek Chabraszewski, Jakub Semeniuk.

Page 11 *Woman in a Poppy Field* (c.1900), Leon Giran-Max
Page 18 *Wheatfield and Cypress Trees* (1889), Vincent Van Gogh
Page 30 *The Fair* (20th century), English School

'Sand' by John Foster (1991) from *Four O'Clock Friday* (Oxford University Press) is included by permission of the
author.

Printed in China

Franklin Watts is a division of Hachette Children's Books, an Hachette UK company.
www.hachette.co.uk

Contents

When I think of summer, I think of fun! Summer is a good time to play outside.

Summer is one of the four seasons of the year – spring, summer, autumn and winter. Summer is the warmest season.

In summer, the sun is strong and high in the sky. The sun rises early in summer and sets late, so the days are long.

Many flowers bloom in the summer sun.

What kinds of flowers make you think of summer?

I like warm days in summer when the sky is clear blue. Sometimes there are fluffy white clouds. Gentle breezes help to keep you cool.

On some days in summer, the weather is humid. The air feels damp and sticky, and there is no wind.

How do you stay cool on hot summer days?

Sometimes in summer there are storms. The clouds are dark, and heavy rain may fall. Have you heard the rumble of thunder in summer?

Why should you stay indoors in a thunderstorm?

In summer, I wear light clothes. When it is really hot, I wear a T-shirt and shorts, and sandals or flip-flops on my feet. A hat helps to keep me cool.

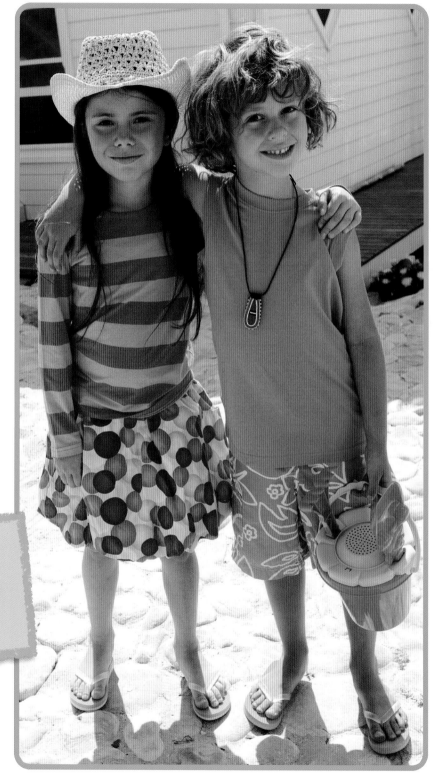

What summer clothes do you wear?

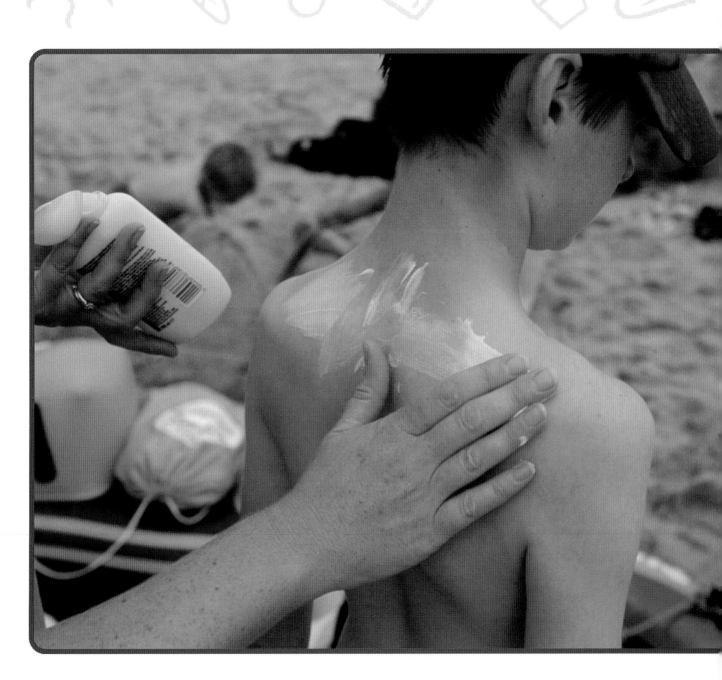

The sun's rays are strong in summer.
I use suncream to stop my skin
burning and don't stay out in the
sun for too long.

In summer, gardens are full of brightly coloured flowers. Plants grow quickly in summer.

If the weather is dry, plants can become thirsty. You may need to water them.

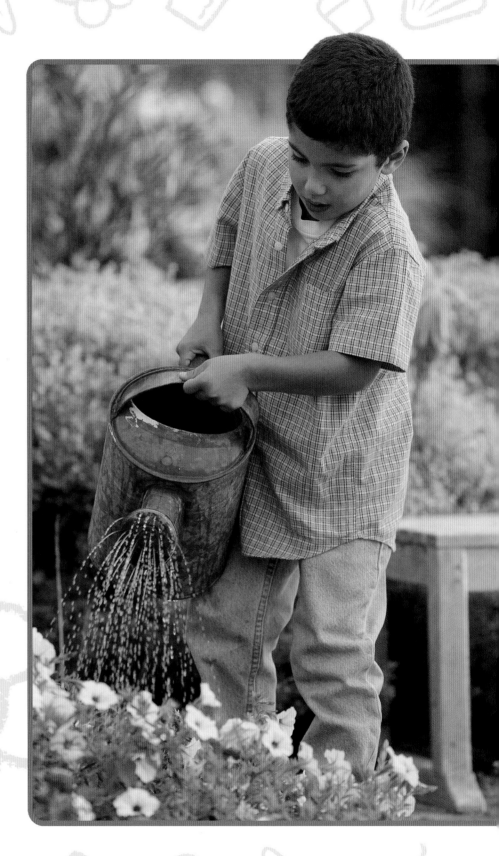

This painting makes me think of fields full of poppies in summer.

Where have you seen wild flowers in summertime?

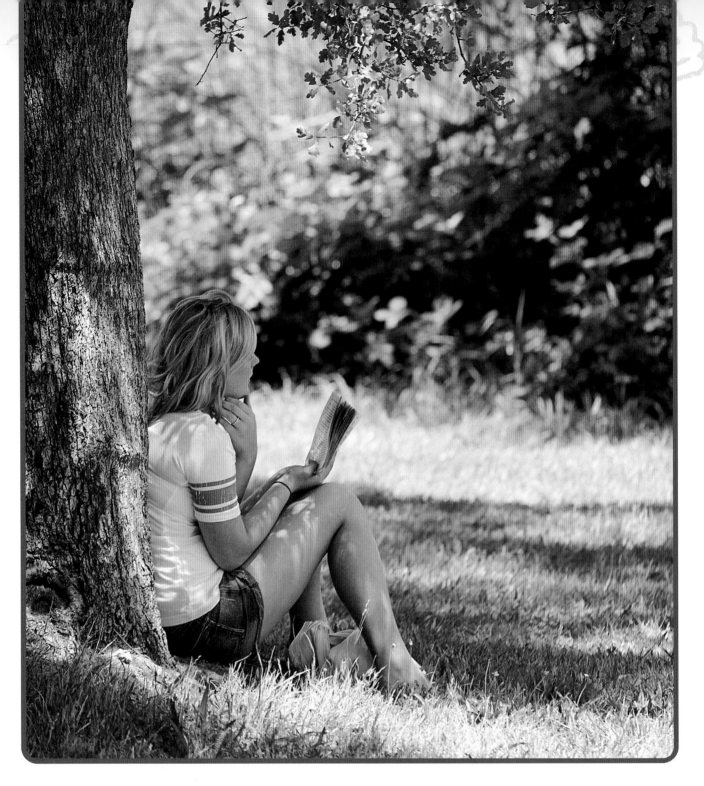

Trees are covered in green leaves in summer. On hot days, I like to relax in the shade of a big tree.

The Beech Tree

I'd like to have a garden
With a beech tree on the lawn;
The little birds that lived there
Would wake me up at dawn.

And in the summer weather
When all the leaves were green,
I'd sit beneath the beech boughs
And see the sky between.

Rose Fyleman

In summer, birds come into my garden to feed on insects and worms. They help gardeners by eating snails and caterpillars, too.

Have you seen birds splashing in water on hot days?

Young frogs and toads come out
of the water in summer.
Birds and foxes like to
eat frogs and toads.

How do you think
frogs and toads
hide from birds
and foxes?

In summer, the air buzzes with the sound of wasps and bees, and I often see butterflies fluttering by.

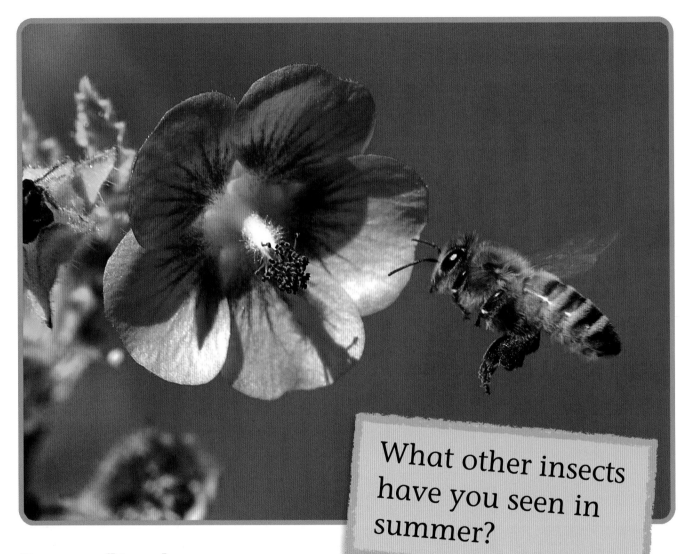

What other insects have you seen in summer?

Butterflies lay eggs, which hatch into caterpillars. Caterpillars love to munch on leaves.

The Caterpillar

Brown and furry
Caterpillar in a hurry
Take your walk
To the shady leaf or stalk.
May no toad spy you,
May the little birds pass by you,
Spin and die,
To live again a butterfly.

Christina Rossetti

Do you know how a caterpillar
becomes a butterfly?

This painting makes me think of fields full of golden wheat. Warm sunshine makes wheat grow really tall.

Have you seen wheat swaying in the summer breeze?

Some crops, such as wheat, maize and oats, become ripe in summer. In late summer, when the crops are fully grown, farmers start to harvest them.

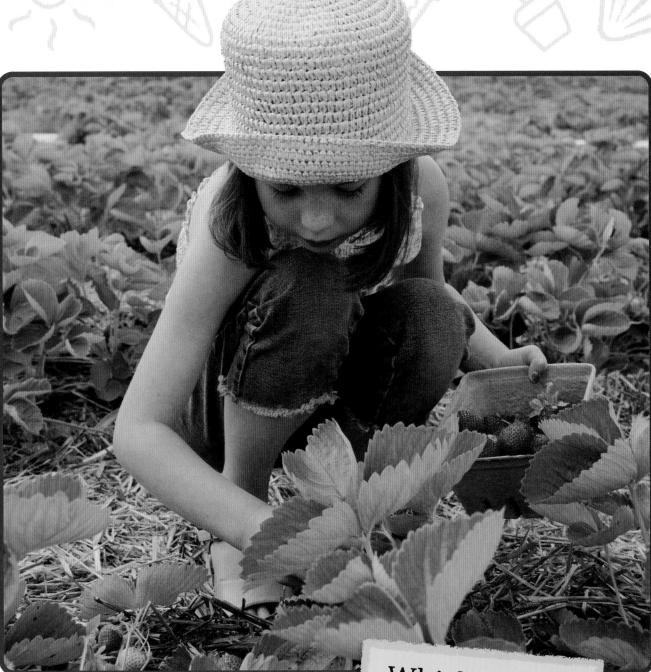

Many kinds of fruit are ready to pick in summer. I love the taste of juicy ripe strawberries.

Which is your favourite summer fruit?

In spring, fruit trees have flowers called blossom. In summer, the blossom becomes young fruit.

Have you seen small apples growing on trees in summer? The apples will be ready to pick in the autumn.

What other kinds of fruit grow on trees?

In the summer sunshine, it's fun to eat outside. We sometimes have barbecues or go to the park for a picnic. I eat lots of fresh salads and vegetables – yum!

What kind of food do you like to eat outside in summer?

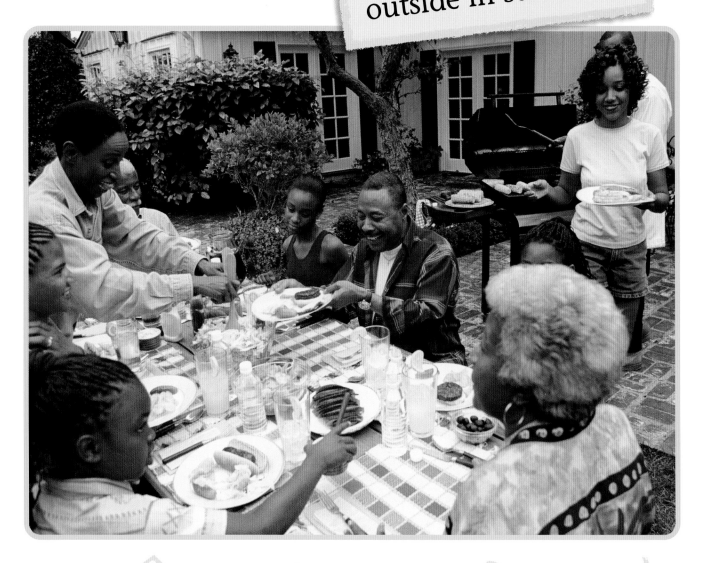

What is your favourite flavour of ice cream?

When it's very hot, I really like eating ice cream. I drink lots of water in summer, too. It helps to keep me cool.

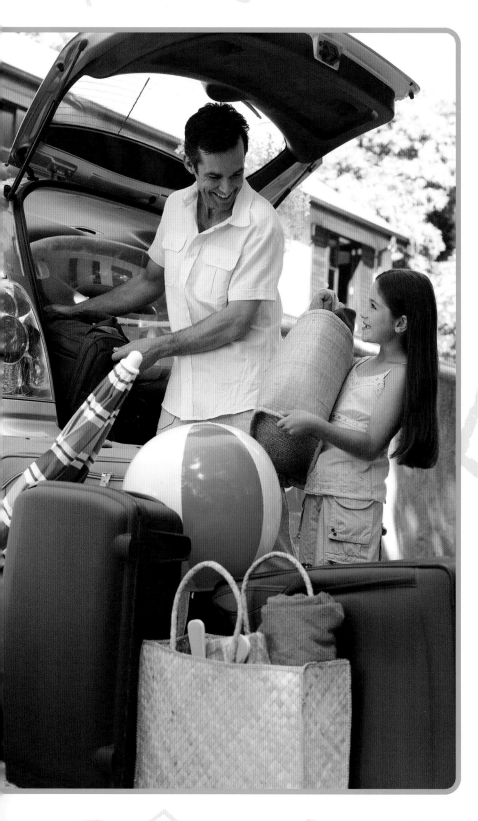

When schools close for the summer, many people go away on holiday.

Roads can become very busy, as lots of cars leave cities and towns.

When I go on holiday I send postcards to my friends.

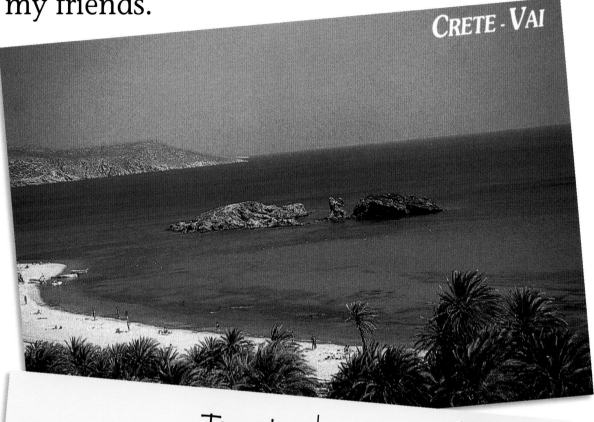

CRETE - VAI

Tuesday

Dear Emily
We are staying in a hotel near the beach. It is very sunny here and the sea is really warm. Today we are going for a ride on a boat!
Love from Alisha xxx

Emily Wells

17 Sandfield Drive

Lower Fenton

GS19 4PL

UK

In summer, I like to play on the beach. I build sandcastles and search for seashells. I jump in waves as they splash against the shore.

What do you like doing on the beach?

Sand

Sand in your fingernails
Sand between your toes
Sand in your earholes
Sand up your nose!

Sand in your sandwiches
Sand on your bananas
Sand in your bed at night
Sand in your pyjamas!

Sand in your sandals
Sand in your hair
Sand in your knickers
Sand everywhere!

John Foster

Does your school have a sports day in summer?

At school in summer, we play tennis and other outdoor sports. At the end of the school term we have a sports day.

The days are long in summer, so I often play outside in the evening. I play football and frisbee and I like to ride my bike.

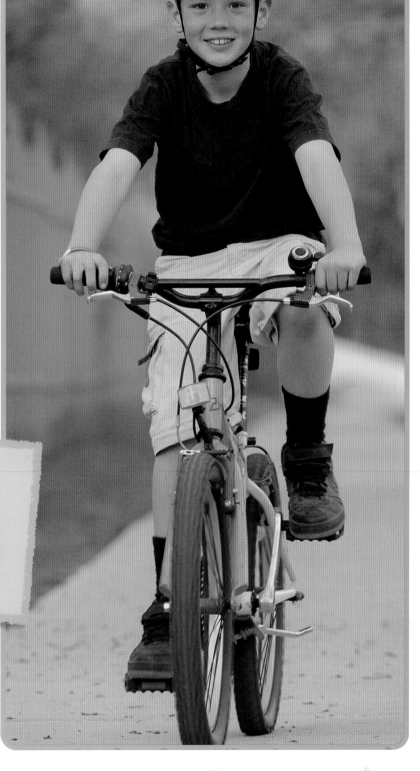

What games and sports do you like playing in summer?

This painting makes me think of summer fairs.

Does the fair ever come to your local town?

In summer, I like to go to carnivals. It's fun to hear the music and watch the dancers. There are lots of special costumes to see.

What do you like doing in summertime? Are there other things that make you think of summer?

Index